25 Days 'Til Christ

An Advent Devotional for the Family

By

Paula Whidden

To read more writing by this author go to www.FaithfulChoices.com.
Thank you for respecting the hard work of this author.

May this little book help draw you closer to Him in ways you didn't know it could. Somehow, through the readings and experiences designed within, may you and your family take steps to have a stronger relationship with Christ this Christmas.

CONTENTS

THE INTRODUCTION

W e begin this journey just after Thanksgiving. Many people call it the season of Advent. In preparation for this time, we will gather supplies. Throughout the 25 days, you and your family will do activities, read Bible verses, eat candy, and appreciate the plan God set in place to reveal how deeply He loves you. You will take steps to make Christ the center of your Christmas.

Items needed:

-5 candles (one white, four others of whatever color you wish) – they can be any size.

-A bag of candy kisses

-Cellophane wrap

-A willing heart and mindThe items listed above aren't necessary, but can be helpful to make your home a place where Christ is central to the Christmas experience. With these items, you will create your own Kiss Calendar and Christmas Candles to help you and your children remember and celebrate. You may also want to make a birthday cake for Christmas day. Any type of cake will do: coffee cake, fluffy cookie, pancakes with a candle, or a traditional birthday cake. You decide. Make it your own.

THE PREP

Today is a day for preparation. As we prepare our homes, let's also prepare our hearts. Before we begin, join me in this prayer:

Lord God Almighty,

Nothing we can do will ever compare to the gift You've given us. And yet, we don't want our minds to wander and get distracted by the things around us. Please use our little attempts at decor to keep our hearts and minds focused on the simple beauty of You. Help us to look at candles and candies as tools to remind us to taste and see how good You really are. Prepare our hearts and minds to see what You want more than what we want.

In Jesus' beautiful name we pray,

Amen.

Now, let's gather the supplies mentioned above and prepare the tools we'll need for the days to come.

1. CHRISTMAS CANDLES

Find a central location in your home and place the candles in a circle formation with the one white candle at the center. We'll call the center candle, the birthday candle. (Some people like to insert them into a wreath, but it isn't strictly necessary.)

Throughout the twenty-five days, we will light one candle a week before Christmas. On Christmas day, we'll light the birthday candle, the white one in the center. They will help us to recall what the Bible means when it refers to Jesus as the light of the world.

"When Jesus spoke again to the people, he said, "I am the light of the world. Whoever follows me will never walk in darkness, but will have the light of life." John 8:12

To help clarify this, I made a video.

Watch it at:
https://www.youtube.com/watch?v=FdqSbjL0ufo&feature=plcp

More prep...

2. KISS CALENDAR

You can make a kiss calendar a couple of ways; the first one involves the cellophane wrap.

Supplies: candy kisses, cellophane, yarn or ribbon, Bible verses found on the last pages of this book.

1. Open the bag of candy kisses

2. Lay out a long piece of cellophane on a table or floor.

3. Make a row of 25 candy kisses on the cellophane leaving space between each for tying on a bow.

4. Print out the verses and cut apart.

5. Fold a Bible verse and place it under or near each kiss.

6. Fold the cellophane over the kisses so that you create a tube of kisses.

7. Using ribbon or yarn, tie a bow between each kiss.

8. Tie off the top and bottom of your strip of kisses with the ribbon or yarn.

9. Hang your Kiss Calendar somewhere you can easily see each day.

You've now made a Kiss Calendar.

If you prefer a simpler approach, you could place 25 kisses into one container on a table with the folded Bible verses in another container.

Eat one kiss and read one Bible verse every day. You could add the personal mom or dad kiss in addition to the chocolate version.

Save the verses and place them in a bag or box to be reused on day 22.

I created another video of me making a kiss calendar if you need further help.

You can see it on my Youtube channel here:

https://www.youtube.com/watch?v=Awv-0WczvOQ&feature=channel&list=UL

3. Extra Activity - The Hunt

This day is meant to help us not just to read the word, but do something with it. You may incorporate it at anytime throughout the 25 Days.

Treasure Hunt

As a family, go for a drive or a walk. Explore your town, neighborhood or local shopping area. Search for the following items. Every time you get one, give yourself the score indicated. Tally them up below. Play on your own or with friends.

For bonus points, guess how these items help us to focus our thoughts on Christ this Christmas. Let's get our imaginations engaged. Enable the members of your family to suggest their own ideas, no answer is wrong. Decide among yourselves who deserves to win.

(Example: I found 5 candy canes, each worth 300 points...total 15 00 points)

Scoring for The Hunt:

Christmas tree (worth 100 points)

Santa (worth 200 points)

Candy Cane (worth 300 points)

Snow/snowflakes (worth 100 points)

Wreath (worth 200 points)

Bows (worth 100 points)

Nativity scene (worth 500 points)

Angels (worth 500 points)

Reindeer (worth 100 points)

Stars (worth 100 points)

Total score:

Declare a winner!

DAY 1: THE WORD
(Candle #1)

We begin by lighting a candle. Pick one of the four candles surrounding the birthday candle to light. We'll read the first part of the story of Christ's birth.

Read aloud.

"In the beginning was the <u>Word</u>, and the <u>Word</u> was with God, and the <u>Word</u> was God. He was with God in the beginning. Through him all things were made; without him nothing was made that has been made. In him was life, and that life was the light of all mankind. The light shines in the darkness, and the darkness has not overcome it." John 1:1-5 NIV

What? There's no baby here? Here, we learned something interesting. Reread the verses above. Wherever a word is underlined, fill in the name Jesus. (It helps to read it out loud.)

At Christmas, we get the same sensation of waiting for a Savior; the Word became flesh (aka. human like you and me). He came to be a light for all mankind. As you look at the flickering candle light before you, take a moment to pray.

Ask God to help you understand Jesus better throughout the next 24 days.

Question of the day:

Is there any part of the story of Christmas you don't understand? Share with your family.

DAY 2: THE SNAKE

God planned to save humanity many years before the baby lay in the manger. He knew what He had in mind to do. He knew His timing. We read of Him voicing His plan in the beginning with Adam and Eve in the garden.

Adam and Eve sinned and got caught. God gave them consequences for their actions, by kicking them out of the garden and making them work for survival. But He also had consequences for the sneaky snake that started the sin ball rolling down the hill.

He told the snake, **"I will put hatred between you and the woman. Your children and her children will be enemies. Her son will crush your head. And you will crush his heel." Genesis 3:15 NIrV**

When God told the snake (also known as Satan) "Her son will crush your head," He meant to inform Satan, in the end, "You lose." God hinted at what will come when Jesus arrives. Still, God was patient and didn't rush His plan.

Question of the day:

What do you think about God's plan? Had you imagined how early it started?

DAY 3: THE BLESSING

In the generations following Adam and Eve, God sent prophets to help the people understand Him. They spoke God's words for the time in which they lived, but they also gave glimpses of God's intent. Step by step, God showed His people who they could expect to come and help them. He prepared them for a Messiah.

(The word, Messiah, is a Hebrew word meaning "Anointed One" or "Chosen One.")

God told Abraham the world would be blessed through his family.

"I will bless those who bless you, and whoever curses you I will curse; and all peoples on earth will be blessed through you." Genesis 12:3 NIV

Once again God gave a hint of what He planned to do.

Historically, no other leader or family member of Abraham (or anyone else) has affected the world the way Jesus has. The impact of Jesus' birth sent ripples through every society on earth for centuries.

Question of the day:

Who is a member of your family you respect and admire?

DAY 4: THE CROWN

As the years pass, God pointed people toward His Messiah. We've learned He had a plan from the beginning. The Messiah would come from Abraham's family which grew bigger and bigger over time.

We read of one part of this huge family in Genesis. A man named Jacob had 11 sons. At one point, God changed Jacob's name to Israel. That's right; this family started the whole country of Israel.

Each son's family became a tribe of Israel named after that son. One of the sons was named Judah. From his name a whole people group emerged. The Jewish people came from this group.

One momentous day, Jacob told his son Judah,

"The right to rule will not leave Judah. The ruler's rod will not be taken from between his feet. It will be his until the king it belongs to comes. It will be his until the nations obey him." **Genesis 49:10 NIV**

Question of the day:

When you think of a king, what do you picture? What does a king do?

DAY 5: THE PUZZLE PIECE

God's pieced together a puzzle. He's filled in clues as to who the people of Israel could expect their Messiah to be. He did it patiently and progressively, leaving little to chance. Who can control what family they come from?

Who can decide where they will be born? These verses matter, because God knew, God planned, and God prepared.

At least 700 years prior to Jesus' birth (in Bethlehem), God told the prophet Micah to share these words with His people:

The Lord says, "Bethlehem, you might not be an important town in the nation of Judah. But out of you will come a ruler over Israel for me. His family line goes back to the early years of your nation. It goes all the way back to days of long ago." Micah 5:2 NIV

No matter what happened in Israel, God made them aware of His plan. He gave them hope, and it (He) would come.

Question of the day:

What makes someone important? Do you think of yourself as important or not? Why?

DAY 6: THE MOM

We don't control where we're born. We certainly cannot pick our parents. But, have I mentioned, God had a plan?

This Messiah would be the light of the world, as God designed from the beginning of the world. He would come from Abraham's family, and more specifically from David's family. He'd be born in Bethlehem. AND, the birth itself would be unique.

Somewhere between 600 and 700 years before the birth of Christ, the prophet Isaiah discovered this piece of God's Messianic puzzle. As Isaiah shared these words, it makes us wonder, how odd it might have sounded in his own ears.

"The Lord himself will give you a miraculous sign. The virgin is going to have a baby. She will give birth to a son. And he will be called Immanuel." Isaiah 7:14 NIV

(FYI – "Immanuel" means "God is with us")

What?

This prophecy might freak out anyone. We will find out later that it really happened.

Question of the day:

Have you ever heard of unusual births? What was the most unusual thing about your birth?

DAY 7: THE PARENTS
(candle #2)

Have you been wondering why we haven't come back to those candles yet? Each week as we approach Christmas, we will light another candle. You may want to relight it throughout the week in anticipation of the arrival of Jesus' birthday.

Today, we'll light a second candle from the outside four. (We're saving the birthday candle for Christmas day.) After we light candle #2, we'll read how Joseph and Mary got informed of their involvement in God's plan.

Read aloud.

1. MARY (the Mom's point of view):

"**God sent the angel Gabriel to Nazareth, a town in Galilee. He was sent to a virgin. The girl was engaged to a man named Joseph. He came from the family line of David. The virgin's name was Mary. The angel greeted her and said, 'The Lord has given you special favor. He is with you.'**

Mary grew very upset because of his words. She wondered what kind of greeting this could be. But the angel said to her, 'Do not be afraid, Mary. God is very pleased with you. You will become pregnant and give birth to a son. You must name him Jesus. He will be great and will be called the Son of the Most High God. The Lord God will make him a king like his father David of long ago. He will rule forever over his people, who came from Jacob's family. His kingdom will never end.'

'How can this happen?'Mary asked the angel. 'I am a virgin.'

19

The angel answered, 'The Holy Spirit will come to you. The power of the Most High God will cover you. So, the holy one that is born will be called the Son of God." Luke 1:26b-35 NIV

Check out Mary's response to this stunning news:

"'I serve the Lord,' Mary answered. 'May it happen to me just as you said it would.' Then the angel left her." Luke 1:38 NIV

2. JOSEPH (the Dad's point of view):

"This is how the birth of Jesus Christ came about. His mother Mary and Joseph had promised to get married. But before they started to live together, it became clear that she was going to have a baby. She became pregnant by the power of the Holy Spirit. Her husband Joseph was a godly man. He did not want to put her to shame in public. So he planned to divorce her quietly."   Matthew 1:18-19 NIV

Don't you just love the honesty of the Bible where it tells us how Jesus' Dad was ready to divorce Mary? There's more to this story...

"But as Joseph was thinking about this, an angel of the Lord appeared to him in a dream. The angel said, 'Joseph, son of David, don't be afraid to take Mary home as your wife. The baby inside her is from the Holy Spirit. She is going to have a son. You must give him the name Jesus. That is because he will save his people from their sins.'

All of this took place to bring about what the Lord had said would happen. He had said through the prophet, 'The virgin is going to have a baby. She will give birth to a son. And he will be called Immanuel.' The name Immanuel means 'God with us.'

Joseph woke up. He did what the angel of the Lord commanded him to do. He took Mary home as his wife. But he did not make love to her until after she gave birth to a son. And Joseph gave him the name Jesus." Matthew 1:20-25 NIV

Imagine the bravery exhibited by Mary and Joseph as they followed God so faithfully.

Question of the day:

Have you ever known any brave parents?

What are the bravest or craziest things your parents have done?

DAY 8: THE SON

God left nothing to doubt. He held back no part of His promise. He wanted to open people's eyes to what He had in mind. He did not send another prophet; Israel could expect no new King. This Messiah would be more than those things.

Though Mary and Joseph got to care for Him, the Messiah would be God's Son. God explained it several hundred years before they ever cuddled a baby and placed him in a manger.

"I will announce what the Lord has promised. He said to me, 'You are my son. Today I have become your father.' " Psalm 2:7 NIV

Knowledge of this prophecy dwelt inside Jesus. When a man named Nicodemus asked how a person could be saved, Jesus said this:

"God loved the world so much that he gave his one and only Son. Anyone who believes in him will not die but will have eternal life. God did not send his Son into the world to judge the world. He sent his Son to save the world through him." John 3:16, 17 NIV

Here, Jesus proclaimed, "I know who I am, you need to know too."

Question of the day:

When you look at nativity scenes or consider Jesus' birthday, how important is it to you that He is God's Son? Why?

DAY 9: THE PROPHECY

Mary and Joseph began the preparations for a new baby. I wonder what they had heard about the Messiah. What did they imagine He would be like?

The prophet Isaiah told people this description many years before the Savior's birth:

"For to us a child is born, to us a son is given, and the government will be on his shoulders. And he will be called Wonderful Counselor, Mighty God, Everlasting Father, Prince of Peace." Isaiah 9:6 NIV

On the plus side, He would be wise, mighty, (fatherly?) and peaceful. On the negative side, "the government will be on his shoulders." That doesn't sound good.

Did you catch the statement? He would be God.

Mary and Joseph's minds already understood this baby would be God, with skin. Wow!

Question of the day:

If you had heard these descriptions before His birth, what assumptions come to your mind?

DAY 10: THE FATHER

If you remember from Isaiah's description of the Messiah yesterday, one of the nicknames applied to Him was "Everlasting Father." It might have been odd for Mary and Joseph to think about their baby as the Everlasting Father. Years later, when Jesus was ministering to people, He referred to God as His heavenly Father. He directly addressed God in prayer as Father several times.

When Jesus taught the disciples, He wasn't confused. Jesus clearly grasped who He was:

"I give them eternal life, and they shall never perish; no one will snatch them out of my hand. My Father, who has given them to me, is greater than all; no one can snatch them out of my Father's hand. I and the Father are one." John 10:28-30 NIV

As we prepare to celebrate Christmas this year, let's remember God's plan to give us an Everlasting Father regardless of the skills found in our earthly fathers. He set the standard for fatherhood.

Question of the day:

How do you think Joseph's stomach felt with this description stuck in his brain?

DAY 11: THE ROCK

Have you ever observed a building when it's under construction? Builders place cement "footers" around the base of a building or they pour a cement foundation.

In Israel, at the time of Jesus' birth, they built with stones. The entire building's strength came from how well the builders placed the first stone. It was the cornerstone of the whole building.

A poorly placed cornerstone could mean a tilted building incapable of weathering a tough storm.

One description of the Messiah, which Mary and Joseph learned from childhood, came from the idea of a cornerstone. The prophet Isaiah described the Messiah this way:

"So this is what the Sovereign LORD says: "See, I lay a stone in Zion (another expression for Israel)**, a tested stone, a precious cornerstone for a sure foundation; the one who relies on it will never be stricken with panic." Isaiah 28:16 NIV** (italics are mine)

In the Psalms it said,

"The stone the builders rejected has become the cornerstone;"Psalm 118:22

Jesus made reference to these verses in His ministry later to confirm how it applied to Him.

Question of the day:

Since Joseph and Mary were taught this reference, what do you think they assumed concerning this future baby?

DAY 12: THE KING

Let's recap:

Mary and Joseph believed the coming baby would be wise, caring, peaceful, strong, fatherly, and like a rock. The book of Psalms also described blessings God had for all nations because of Him. All kings would submit to Him.

"Then all nations will be blessed through him, and they will call him blessed." Psalm 72:17b NIV

"May all kings bow down to him and all nations serve him." Psalm 72:11 NIV

The book of Revelation puts it simply:

"On his robe and on his thigh he has this name written: KING OF KINGS AND LORD OF LORDS." Revelation 19:16 NIV

That's who this baby is. If we put it in our terms, we'd call Him: the Boss of Bosses, Master of Masters, or President of Presidents.

Question of the day:

Do you think Mary and Joseph were nervous about their role in the future of all people? Why?

DAY 13: THE LIGHTS
ACTIVITY DAY

LIGHT COUNT

You'll set a timer for 1 minute. Search your home and count all the lights you find. Do this on your own or as a competition with friends or family. How many lights did you find? The winner is the one who finds the most. If you have many great counters in your family, try timing them.

(Want a bigger challenge? Count the lights in your neighborhood.)

Read these verses and consider the lights you found.

Jesus -- the Light of the World:

"The true light that gives light to everyone was coming into the world." John 1:9

"When Jesus spoke again to the people, he said, "I am the light of the world. Whoever follows me will never walk in darkness, but will have the light of life." John 8:12

Us -- as we share His light:

"You are the light of the world. A town built on a hill cannot be hidden." Matthew 5:14

Question of the day:

What do you think it means to be the light of the world? Why?

DAY 14: THE WISE MEN
(Candle #3)

Today, we'll light three of the candles surrounding the birthday candle.

We've already unearthed:

God planned for Jesus' arrival from the beginning. He invited Mary and Joseph into His plan. There were others also waiting, seeking, learning, and ready to step out in faith in an amazing way.

Read these verses aloud.

"After Jesus' birth, wise men from the east came to Jerusalem. They asked, "Where is the child who has been born to be king of the Jews? When we were in the east, we saw his star. Now we have come to worship him." Matthew 2:1, 2 NIV

These wise men got involved in God's plan long before they arrived. They possibly served as advisors to a king; they studied and learned about the stars, about how they affected people. They had also discovered the prophecies about the Messiah. They acknowledged God's power and wanted to meet His Messiah, even though they lived in the East, maybe as far as Persia. They left their comfortable lives to cross a desolate desert in search of a baby. They already understood He would be a baby. Now that's faith!

(By the way, the Bible never tells us how many wise men came. They brought three presents, but the presents may have been given by two or twelve. We'll talk more about this later.)

Question of the day:

What does faith mean to you?

DAY 15: THE ESCAPE

We often put Mary, Joseph, and Jesus into a sweet package as a contented little family. But Jesus' story is full of gut wrenching heart ache, even in the beginning.

Those wise men travelled to see Him, but first they stopped to meet the local King, Herod. They asked for further guidance on their journey. Herod heard the predictions of the Messiah. He believed the baby would become a King. To Herod's way of thinking, this baby came to take his job. He thought the Messiah would dethrone him. Herod planned to stop that at any cost.

As a result, Herod decided to kill all the baby boys in Israel who were 0-2 years old, because he wasn't certain of the baby's age. This tragic period in Israel's history marked the first years of Jesus life. Yet, God's plan remained intact.

"When they had gone, an angel of the Lord appeared to Joseph in a dream. 'Get up,' he said, 'take the child and his mother and escape to Egypt. Stay there until I tell you, for Herod is going to search for the child to kill him.' " Matthew 2:13

From the very beginning, Jesus encountered struggles in life. As we face difficulties, we can look to our Savior with the realization that He understands our problems. He's had them too.

Question of the day:

What problem could you bring to Jesus? Talk to Him in prayer and share it, knowing and trusting He understands it.

DAY 16: THE WAITERS

HIM:

It wasn't just the wise men who dreamt of the Messiah's arrival. Other people waited expectantly for Him, one such person was Simeon. He believed God wanted him to meet the Messiah before his life finished. Though he was old, he eagerly waited at the Temple in Jerusalem. Eight days after Jesus' birth, Mary and Joseph brought Him to be dedicated, and they ran into Simeon.

"In Jerusalem there was a man named Simeon. He was a good and godly man. He was waiting for God's promise to Israel to happen. The Holy Spirit was with him. The Spirit had told Simeon that he would not die before he had seen the Lord's Christ. The Spirit led him into the temple courtyard.

Then Jesus' parents brought the child in. They came to do for him what the Law required. Simeon took Jesus in his arms and praised God. He said, 'Lord, you are the King over all. Now let me, your servant, go in peace. That is what you promised. My eyes have seen your salvation. You have prepared it in the sight of all people. It is a light to be given to those who aren't Jews. It will bring glory to your people Israel.'

The child's father and mother were amazed at what was said about him. Then Simeon blessed them. He said to Mary, Jesus' mother, 'This child is going to cause many people in Israel to fall and to rise. God has sent him. But many will speak against him. The thoughts of many hearts will be known. A sword will wound your own soul too.' " Luke 2:25-35 NIV

Just eight days into this tiny life, Mary and Joseph encountered someone who had expected God's plan, just as they had.

HER:

On the same day they met Simeon, Mary and Joseph also bumped into another person who had been aware of God's details. Her name was Anna. She was an elderly woman who remained at the temple praying and worshipping continually, since she no longer had family.

Mary and Joseph have arrived at the temple ready to follow the Jewish rules for a male child, and Anna approached them.

"There was also a prophet named Anna. She was the daughter of Penuel from the tribe of Asher. Anna was very old. After getting married, she lived with her husband seven years. Then she was a widow until she was 84. She never left the temple. She worshiped night and day, praying and going without eating.

Anna came up to Jesus' family at that very moment. She gave thanks to God. And she spoke about the child to all who were looking forward to the time when Jerusalem would be set free." Luke 2:36-38 NIV

We often think about Christmas as a time for family. What we imagine centers on the people who raised us and gave us birth. With Anna's revelation, we witness how God's plan isn't about our household family, but about His family.

Anna had no one with whom to celebrate this knowledge God placed in her head. She was alone. Yet, the joy of this first Christmas came to her personally. Like Anna, when we become adopted into God's family by accepting the gift of Christ, He never leaves us alone at Christmas or any other time.

Questions of the Day:

How do you think this made Mary and Joseph feel? Why?

How do you find joy when you're alone?

(Consider doing something to care for people who may be alone: older people who live in care facilities, people in the hospital, or maybe someone you know personally.)

DAY 17: THE LAMB

The birthday we celebrate on Christmas is important, not just because of the miracle of the baby, but because of the life and sacrifice of the man. He started life as we all do, with the slow steps of an infant. When He reached the age of maturity, it was time for Him to face the world as a man. The ministry of Christ was about to begin.

To initiate this leg of the journey, He went into the desert and got baptized by John. John had become respected by many people as a prophet of God. When Jesus approached, we read John's first reaction to His presence:

"The next day John saw Jesus coming toward him and said, "Look, the Lamb of God, who takes away the sin of the world!" John 1:29

By saying this, John exposed Jesus' purpose. The expression, "Lamb of God," instantly made the people of Israel think of Moses. It reminded them of the lamb they sacrificed each year in memory of the 10th plague mentioned in the book of Exodus.

By sacrificing to God the best lamb they owned, it showed how much they trusted Him. They gave their best to Him. As a result, the first born children were saved.

Now, God was returning the favor. He was giving His best for them, and ultimately for all of us. As a result, all who acknowledge this and give their best to Him also get saved from eternal separation from God.

Question of the Day:

What thoughts come to mind when you think of Jesus (the baby/the man) coming as a sacrifice for you?

DAY 18: THE SPEECH

We've addressed many people and how they responded to the arrival of Jesus. Even if every person on the planet believed in His strength and power, it wouldn't matter; unless it was true. How can we determine the truth?

If Jesus is from God, let's go to source. What are God's words about this? Does He say anything?

As startling as it must have been, the Bible records God's spoken word on the subject:

"As soon as Jesus was baptized, he went up out of the water. At that moment heaven was opened, and he saw the Spirit of God descending like a dove and alighting on him. And a voice from heaven said, 'This is my Son, whom I love; with him I am well pleased.'" Matthew 3:16, 17

When we acknowledge who Jesus really is, the importance of His birthday builds. People have talked about it, prayed for it, imagined it, and dreamt of it. At His arrival, a new world came. More than any other person in history, Jesus' affect on mankind explodes throughout people groups, countries, and continents. Why? Because of who He is and what He did.

Question of the Day:

When you think about Jesus' impact on the world, what matters most to you?

DAY 19 – THE GIFTS
Activity Day

GIFT TIME

Let's make a present for Jesus. It is His birthday we celebrate on Christmas, what can we give Him? Since He's God, He doesn't need anything. But there is something He wants. He wants us.

Write down things you can do or give to Jesus. Some ideas might include: energy, cooking for someone in need, giving money to church, sharing clothes with people who need them, time, etc. Make this real and personal. Come up with as many ideas as you can. Put the papers in a package of some sort. Wrap it and label it "To: Jesus" and "From: your name".

In another box or package, place the verses you've collected from the kiss calendar. Label this package, "From: God" and "To: you or your family."

Place both presents under the tree or wherever you put presents to be opened Christmas day.

Make a game of opening God's present to us by wrapping it with several layers of paper. Then, put on some music and play musical unwrap on Christmas Day. One layer gets removed when the music stops, much like musical chairs, but move the present instead of the people. The winner can then read the verses contained in this package to remind the family of God's gift to us all. If your winner is too young to read it, let someone else have that honor.

DAY 20: THE SHEPHERDS
(Candle #4)

We've been lighting the candles progressively each Sunday as we approach Christmas. Today, it's time for number 4. Be sure to light the previous three candles too. After you light the fourth candle, read these verses about some of the first people to stare into the eyes of Christ.

Read these verses aloud.

"And there were shepherds living out in the fields nearby, keeping watch over their flocks at night. An angel of the Lord appeared to them, and the glory of the Lord shone around them, and they were terrified. But the angel said to them, 'Do not be afraid. I bring you good news that will cause great joy for all the people. Today in the town of David a Savior has been born to you; he is the Messiah, the Lord. This will be a sign to you: You will find a baby wrapped in cloths and lying in a manger.'

Suddenly a great company of the heavenly host appeared with the angel, praising God and saying, 'Glory to God in the highest heaven, and on earth peace to those on whom his favor rests.'

When the angels had left them and gone into heaven, the shepherds said to one another, 'Let's go to Bethlehem and see this thing that has happened, which the Lord has told us about.'

So they hurried off and found Mary and Joseph, and the baby, who was lying in the manger. When they had seen him, they spread the word concerning what had been told them about this child, and all who heard it were amazed at what the shepherds said to them. But Mary treasured up all these things and pondered them in her

heart. The shepherds returned, glorifying and praising God for all the things they had heard and seen, which were just as they had been told." Luke 2:8-20 NIV

Shepherds are regular, hard working, and sweaty men. To these sheep scented individuals, God sent an army of angels. This is the largest group of angels specifically mentioned anywhere within scripture. It's overwhelming to imagine. Previous times in the Bible where someone came face to face with an angel, they shook in their skin. These shepherds get a whole company of angels. Wow!

Without hesitation, the shepherds searched for the baby Messiah. Then, they spread the word of Him. In years to come, Jesus got called the "Good Shepherd." Ironically, His first visitors came from that line of work.

As we see the glowing candles before us, we can remember Jesus, the Light of the World and how He wants us to shine with His light also. The shepherds let their light shine when they fearlessly told everyone of the miraculous baby. We do the same by sharing Jesus' story with our friends. When we invite them to church, maybe to a Christmas service, and we tell others how His life affects ours, we continue their story.

"Neither do people light a lamp and put it under a bowl. Instead they put it on its stand, and it gives light to everyone in the house. In the same way, let your light shine before others, that they may see your good deeds and glorify your Father in heaven." Matthew 5:15, 16 NIV

Question of the Day:

How can we imitate the shepherds today and let our light shine?

DAY 21: THE NAMES

As He grew, Jesus developed many nicknames. For the people of this time, a name expressed your personality and who you will be. Here is a list of some names applied to Jesus:

• Son of God

• The Christ (Greek for "anointed One")

• The Messiah (Hebrew for "anointed One")

• Mighty God

• Everlasting Father

• Prince of Peace

• Wonderful Counselor

• Lord

• Rabbi (which means teacher)

• Creator

• Almighty

• First and Last

• The Life

• Bread of Life

• The Word

• Son of David

25 Days 'Til Christ

•Prophet

•Servant

•Good Shepherd (caregiver)

•Lamb of God (sacrificing Himself)

•The Way

•The Truth

Phew! That's a bundle of names. Which is your favorite? Why?

As we think about Christmas, let's consider these names and what they mean. They help us to understand Jesus better.

Questions of the Day:

What does your name mean?

If you never searched for the meaning previously, take a moment to look it up, Google it or ask a parent. Does your name describe you?

Do you have any nicknames? How many?

DAY 22: THE FIRST NAME

The name "Jesus" has great depth and meaning all by itself. God picked out this name and told Mary and Joseph to give it to the Messiah. The name Jesus means "one who saves."

There's something about the name "Jesus" which the Bible tells us is unique. When someone gets baptized, they do so in the name of Jesus. When someone prays in the name of Jesus, people get healed. Demons are cast out of people in the name of Jesus. We are saved in the name of Jesus.

Philippians 2:9-11 puts it this way:

"Therefore God exalted him to the highest place and gave him the name that is above every name, that at the name of Jesus every knee should bow, in heaven and on earth and under the earth, and every tongue acknowledge that Jesus Christ is Lord, to the glory of God the Father."

Now that's one amazing name!

Question of the Day:

Have you met anyone with an unusual name? What is it?

DAY 23: THE PAIN

We're getting close; His birthday is only a few days away. Are you feeling the anticipation and excitement?

As we've been studying God's plan, we discovered how early God set forth his plan for mankind. We examined the nuggets of truth God doled out over hundreds of years before the birth of Jesus. We discussed how this one man fulfilled each prophecy concerning his birth and his life. But that's not all.

Jesus didn't live for His own enjoyment; He existed to fulfill the plan. He sacrificed Himself for us. Like the lamb at Passover, Jesus gave His life for ours. Isaiah exposed these details hundreds of years before the baby's birth.

"Surely he took up our pain and bore our suffering, yet we considered him punished by God, stricken by him, and afflicted. But he was pierced for our transgressions, he was crushed for our iniquities; the punishment that brought us peace was on him, and by his wounds we are healed. We all, like sheep, have gone astray, each of us has turned to our own way; and the LORD has laid on him the iniquity of us all." Isaiah 53:4-6 NIV

Question of the Day:

After reading these things, what would you say to Jesus if you could talk with Him today?

DAY 24: THE GIFT

"Only two more shopping days until Christmas," the advertisements declare. We want to give and receive. In the mix of presents and toys or lack of them, we sometimes forget the real gift of Christmas.

All this time, we've studied about who Jesus is, but do we grasp *what* Jesus is?

He's God's gift to us. The best gift we will ever receive.

"For God so loved the world that he gave his one and only Son, that whoever believes in him shall not perish but have eternal life. For God did not send his Son into the world to condemn the world, but to save the world through him." John 3:16-17 NIV

Because of this gift, we gain access to God's family.

"Yet to all who did receive him, to those who believed in his name, he gave the right to become children of God" John 1:12

As one domino falls on another, so becoming part of His family excites us. We yearn for more people to become family members too. As a result, we share His story, like the shepherds, with anyone we can.

Question of the Day:

Do you attend church? If not, what's holding you back?

If so, when was the last time you invited someone to join you at church? Think of someone and invite them.

THE PARTY PREP
Prepare to Celebrate...

Imagine the most important person in history is coming to your home tomorrow. He's your personal friend. What would you do to prepare for His arrival?

Decide for yourself something to do to prepare for the special day; the day we've adopted to celebrate His arrival among us. Go to a special church service. Write a note to God. Why not throw a birthday party?

When we celebrate a birthday, we decorate, clean, cook, and play games. Whether it's big or small, let's plan a party for Jesus. Place streamers across the ceiling. Make or purchase birthday signs. Make or purchase a birthday cake.

Is your heart pounding with anticipation yet?

If life's been tough lately, it may help to remember the truth of the moment. The only people in Bethlehem ready for the Messiah's arrival were Mary and Joseph.

They travelled for days, walking through dirt toward the town of Bethlehem. When they came into town, they hunted for a hotel room. They discovered what God often finds when He knocks at the door of our hearts. There was no room. The Messiah entered the world homeless.

Jesus wants to be invited into your life too. If you've never done this before, take a moment to pray. Ask Him to come into your life. Let Him know that you want Him to be the Boss of Bosses in your life. He isn't pushy. He doesn't force Himself on us. He waits for our invitation.

DAY 25: THE DAY

It's here!

It's Jesus' birthday; the only birth still celebrated 2000 years after the fact. If we celebrated it the way He deserves, the birthday candles would look like a bon fire. But, this baby we remember in our manger scene isn't a baby any more. He's the Wonderful Counselor, Mighty God, Everlasting Father, and Prince of Peace. In the beginning, He was with God and He was God. Jesus is the Word of God, made flesh.

Let's eat cake, light the Birthday candle, play a game, open the present from Jesus. Let's remember His small beginning, and how the world changed. He brought love, joy, peace, patience, kindness, goodness, faithfulness, gentleness and self-control. He spreads them around the world through all those who let Him lead their lives.

Here's how it all started: (Light the 4 candles plus the Birthday candle)

Read the story aloud as a family…

"In those days Caesar Augustus issued a decree that a census should be taken of the entire Roman world. (This was the first census that took place while Quirinius was governor of Syria.) And everyone went to their own town to register.

So Joseph also went up from the town of Nazareth in Galilee to Judea, to Bethlehem the town of David, because he belonged to the house and line of David. He went there to register with Mary, who was pledged to be married to him and was expecting a child. While they were there, the time came for the baby to be born, and she gave birth to her firstborn, a son. She wrapped him in cloths

and placed him in a manger, because there was no guest room available for them." Luke 2:1-7 NIV

Question of the Day:

How has this simple day changed your life?

KISS CALENDAR (THE BIBLE VERSES)

(CUT OUT EACH VERSE, FOLD IT, AND PLACE IT WITH A CANDY KISS IN YOUR KISS CALENDAR.)

John 1:1, 2 "In the beginning was the Word, and the Word was with God, and the Word was God. He was with God in the beginning."

John 1:3, 4"Through him all things were made; without him nothing was made that has been made. In him was life, and that life was the light of all mankind."

John 1:9 "The true light that gives light to everyone was coming into the world."

John 1:14 "The Word became flesh and made his dwelling among us. We have seen his glory, the glory of the one and only Son, who came from the Father, full of grace and truth."

Isaiah 7:14 "Therefore the Lord himself will give you a sign: The virgin will conceive and give birth to a son, and will call him Immanuel."

Isaiah 9:6 "For to us a child is born, to us a son is given, and the government will be on his shoulders. And he will be called Wonderful Counselor, Mighty God, Everlasting Father, Prince of Peace."

Luke 1:30 "But the angel said to her, "Do not be afraid, Mary; you have found favor with God."

Luke 1:31 "You will conceive and give birth to a son, and you are to call him Jesus."

Luke 1:32a "He will be great and will be called the Son of the Most High."

Luke 2:11 "Today in the town of David a Savior has been born to you; he is the Messiah, the Lord."

Luke 2:14 "Glory to God in the highest heaven, and on earth peace to those on whom his favor rests."

Acts 4:12 "Salvation is found in no one else, for there is no other name under heaven given to mankind by which we must be saved."

Isaiah 53:4 "Surely he took up our pain and bore our suffering, yet we considered him punished by God, stricken by him, and afflicted."

Isaiah 53:5 "But he was pierced for our transgressions, he was crushed for our iniquities; the punishment that brought us peace was on him, and by his wounds we are healed."

Galatians 4:4 "But when the set time had fully come, God sent his Son, born of a woman, born under the law,"

John 1:12 "Yet to all who did receive him, to those who believed in his name, he gave the right to become children of God"

John 3:16 "For God so loved the world, that he gave his one and only son that whoever believes in him shall not perish but have eternal life."

John 15:1 "I am the true vine, and my Father is the gardener."

John 3:17 "For God did not send his Son into the world to condemn the world, but to save the world through him."

John 16:51 "I am the living bread that came down from heaven. Whoever eats this bread will live forever. This bread is my flesh, which I will give for the life of the world."

Philippians 2:9-11 ""Therefore God exalted him to the highest place and gave him the name that is above every name, that at the name of Jesus every knee should bow, in heaven and on earth and under the earth, and every tongue acknowledge that Jesus Christ is Lord, to the glory of God the Father."

Matthew 3:17 "And a voice from heaven said, 'This is my Son, whom I love; with him I am well pleased.' "

John 11:25 "Jesus said to her, "I am the resurrection and the life. The one who believes in me will live, even though they die"

John 10:11 "I am the good shepherd. The good shepherd lays down his life for his sheep."

John 14:6 "Jesus answered, 'I am the way, the truth and the life. no one comes to the Father except through me."

ABOUT THE AUTHOR

Paula Whidden studied at Fuller Theological Seminary to receive her Masters of Divinity degree. Soon after, God opened the door for her to do church ministry as a Youth Pastor at First Baptist Church of Sunland in Sunland, California. She adored sharing the hope of heaven with the teens, believing she'd do this forever.

But, when she became a wife and mom, she noticed a need among the children of the community; she transitioned to become a Children's Pastor. She eventually became a Children's Ministry Director at Real Life Church in Santa Clarita, one of the fastest growing churches in America, but life changed.

A passion grew within her to help parents and adults. She began writing online at www.Examiner.com as their Los Angeles Faith and Family Examiner. She started her own website, www.FaithfulChoices.com. Now, she writes every day in the hopes of enabling people to see how the choices we make affect our destination. She loves to help families find joy, one faithful choices at a time.

If you want to read more by this author visit

www.FaithfulChoices.com

Paula's next book *Couple Corners: 52 Faithful Choices for a More Joy-Filled Marriage* will be available later in December 2013.

SPECIAL THANKS

Thank you to my wonderful family who patiently allowed me to stay at the computer, and type this when they'd like to play instead. Tim, you never fail to support and encourage. Bethany and Rachel, our hugs each day fill me up and enable me to give to others. Without you, nothing would or could happen.

Thank you to my friends, who placed me and this book before God, trusting His will for whatever may happen.

Most of all thank you for my loving Savior who rescued me years ago, and daily forgives my messed up soul. I'm so glad you gave up the beauty of heaven to be a baby and serve me.

www.ingramcontent.com/pod-product-compliance
Lightning Source LLC
Chambersburg PA
CBHW060042040426
42331CB00032B/2149